red wine

discovering, exploring, enjoying

red wine

discovering, exploring, enjoying

Jonathan Ray

photography by Alan Williams

RYLAND
PETERS
& SMALL
London New York

For David, Jamie and Tom.

Designer   Luis Peral-Aranda
Consultant Editor   Anne Ryland
Editor   Maddalena Bastianelli
Editorial Assistant   Miriam Hyslop
Production   Gavin Bradshaw
Art Director   Gabriella Le Grazie
Publishing Director   Alison Starling

Indexer   Hilary Bird

First published in the USA in 2001
by Ryland Peters & Small, Inc
519 Broadway, 5th Floor,
New York, NY 10012
www.rylandpeters.com

10 9 8

ISBN 1 84172 154 9

Printed in China.

Contents

Introduction

What could be more enjoyable than exploring the world of wine? After all, there can be few other subjects that consider uncorking a bottle and pouring yourself a glass to be an obligatory part of your research.

To the uninitiated, wine might seem a daunting subject best left to wealthy connoisseurs, but in truth it is accessible to everyone, and the basics can be learned in a matter of a few pleasurable hours.

Wine is no more than fermented grape juice, and while climate, soil, and methods of production all make significant contributions to the way a wine tastes, the most important factor by far is the grape itself. The best place to start, therefore, is by learning to identify the most popular grape varieties and by tasting the different wines that they make.

The purpose of this book is to lead you gently by the hand on your journey of discovery, by introducing you to the major red grape varieties, and by explaining a bit about how to store wine, how to serve it, and how to taste it. It will also help you decide which dishes go well with which wines, and it will guide you through the intricacies of restaurant wine lists.

But whereas this book can teach you the difference between Bordeaux and burgundy or port and madeira, only by tasting the wines for yourself can you decide which you prefer, so don't forget to keep a corkscrew handy.

bottle shapes and sizes

The regular wine bottle is standardized the world over at 75 cl. Other sizes such as half bottles (37.5 cl), liter bottles (100 cl), and magnums (150 cl) are also often seen. The general rule of thumb is that the larger the bottle, the more slowly the wine within it will mature—and the longer it will keep—owing to the ratio of wine to oxygen in the bottle.

The two main shapes of bottle for red wines are those common to Bordeaux—green with high shoulders—or Burgundy and the Rhône—greenish-brown with sloping shoulders.

As a rule, Californian and Australian varietals such as Cabernet Sauvignon, Merlot, and Shiraz come in Bordeaux-style bottles, as do Zinfandel, Chianti, and some Riojas.

Beaujolais, California Pinot Noir, big Italians such as Barolo and Barbaresco, Rhônes, Syrah, and some Spanish wines come in Burgundy-style bottles.

Port bottles are made of opaque black glass with high shoulders and a long, thick neck.

"…the larger the bottle the more slowly the wine within it will mature"

Although idiosyncratic designs are now a regular feature of wine bottles, the shape and color of the bottle are still good— but not official—indications of the wine's origin.

labels explained

In essence, wine labels are no different from the labels to be found on cans of baked beans or jars of jelly: they are there to give you all the information you need to make an informed decision about whether or not to buy the product.

A wine label on the front of a bottle must, legally, tell you:

the wine's name

the size of the bottle

the vintage (if there is one)

the wine's alcoholic strength

the producer's name and address

the name of the bottler (if different from the producer)

the name of the shipper (if different from the importer)

the name of the importer

the wine's quality level

where the wine was bottled

country of origin

type of wine

what region and appellation the wine is from

some labels also include the grape variety

Wine imported into the United States, or exported from there, is also obliged to state whether or not sulfur dioxide was used in its production, and to display a government health warning concerning the hazards of drinking wine. (If only the French or Italians would consider displaying a similar label extolling the benefits...)

The statement *"mis(e) en bouteille(s) au château"* on a bottle of French wine indicates that the wine was bottled at the property where it was made.

As a rule, New World producers market their wines by grape variety, while the Europeans tend not to (although this is changing), so it helps to know which varieties make which wines.

While front labels are strictly regulated, back labels (an optional extra) often give a fuller explanation of the wine. Such labels might tell you what foods go well with the wine, how long it should be kept, when it should be opened, what temperature it should be served at, and so on. Neck labels are sometimes added, stating the vintage, some special feature about the wine, or displaying an award won.

single varietals
and blends

To put it at its simplest, wine is no more than the fermented juice of grapes.

A blended wine is one where the fermented juice of one variety is joined with that of another—or others—as in Bordeaux, where any given red wine might be a blend of up to five different varieties, or in the southern Rhône, where Châteauneuf-du-Pape can be made from up to thirteen permitted varieties.

Blending can also encompass different vintages, as with ports or standard red Bordeaux, blended in such a way to make sure they always taste the same.

Strictly speaking, a single varietal is a wine made from one grape variety only. However, rules differ from region to region, and in truth, a single varietal might contain a small amount of another variety. For example, in Australia 80 percent of the wine must come from the named variety, while in the U.S. it is 75 percent.

It used to be that most New World wines were single varietals while those from the Old World were blends, but this distinction is now blurred. What remains true is that some producers prefer the purity and intensity of

single varietals while others believe that careful blending leads to greater subtlety and delicacy.

In Europe the trend has been to name the wines after the region of origin rather than after the variety. It is here that it pays to have a little knowledge: if, for example, you know that you like single varietal Pinot Noirs from Oregon, say, then it is helpful to know that all red burgundies, such as Pommard, Vosne-Romanée, or Aloxe Corton, for example, are also single varietals, being 100 percent Pinot Noir.

There are strong arguments both for blends and for single varietals, arguments that get trotted out whenever two or more winemakers are gathered together. Neither style is better than the other; they are just different, that is all.

cabernet sauvignon

This wine is instantly recognizable in the glass owing to its overwhelming aroma of black currants, its juicy, jammy flavors, and its structure, tannin levels, and complexity. It has the ability to age exceptionally well.

While Cabernet Sauvignon is the most important variety in Bordeaux, it is never used on its own there, producers believing that its qualities can only be enhanced by blending it with one or more of the Cabernet Franc, Malbec, Merlot, Petit Verdot, quartet.

Okay, this is the big one! Cabernet Sauvignon is, without doubt, the most cherished red grape variety in the world, acclaimed as the backbone behind the finest red wines of Bordeaux, and producer of the New World's finest single varietals.

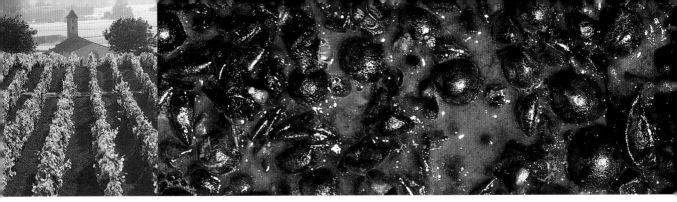

Cabernet Sauvignon is grown throughout Europe, with Bulgaria in particular making excellent single varietals and blends in Suhindol. In Italy it is grown in Piedmont and Emilia-Romagna, and is used to great effect in Tuscany. It is also becoming popular in Spain, where it is often blended with Tempranillo.

It was Cabernet Sauvignon that first brought California to the attention of the wine world, with the best examples usually coming from the Napa Valley and Sonoma County. Hitherto it has often been made as a single varietal (although many "100 percent Cabernet Sauvignons" include tiny amounts of Merlot and Cabernet Franc), but producers have recently been moving away from single varietals toward making so-called Meritage blends, similar in style to Bordeaux, and insisting on using French oak, too. Some producers even use Cabernet Sauvignon to make fortified port-style wines.

In Australia, Cabernet Sauvignon becomes more black currantlike than ever, and is usually blended with Shiraz or Merlot—Coonawarra in South East Australia being the most favored spot for growing the variety. Chile produces some of the finest Cabernet Sauvignons (from pre-phylloxera vines, see page 61), which are exquisitely dark and intense with extraordinary depth. Lighter wines of good— rather than great—quality are also now made in New Zealand and South Africa.

Cabernet Sauvignon in all its forms goes well with roasted meat, steak, game, and most cheese.

merlot

In the Médoc area of Bordeaux, Merlot is very much the junior partner to Cabernet Sauvignon's chairman of the board, being used in blends to soften the latter's dominance. On the right-hand side of the River Garonne, however, in St. Émilion, Pomerol, Fronsac, Bourg, and Blaye, it plays by far the greater role.

Merlot is increasingly being grown in the currently fashionable Languedoc-Roussillon, and is an important grape in northeastern Italy, especially in Friuli, Emilia-Romagna, Trentino-Alto Adige, and the Veneto, and is often a component of the "Super Tuscans," being blended with Sangiovese and Cabernet Sauvignon. At its lowest level, however, Italian Merlots can be unwelcomingly thin and light-bodied with alarmingly high acidity.

In the New World, unblended Merlot can make wines of great style. It is argued that North America's best Merlot comes from Washington State, but it is increasing in popularity in California, too, California Merlots being heavier and fuller than those of Bordeaux. In South America, Argentina makes some very good Merlots, and those of Chile are especially silky and elegant, although they tend not to age quite so well.

Even though many people believed that New Zealand was suited to making only white wine, Merlot has recently become a great success. Plantings in Australia are limited, with producers and consumers seeming to prefer Shiraz for single varietals or Cabernet Sauvignon for blends.

Merlot is grown more or less everywhere that Cabernet Sauvignon is. It is a crucial part of the blends that make up the red Bordeaux, while in the New World it makes top-quality single varietals.

Merlot from whatever country is ideal with any poultry dishes, simply cooked lamb, and soft cheese.

pinot noir

Pinot Noir has been grown in Burgundy for centuries and—unblended—makes the region's world-famous red wines such as Clos de Vougeot, Corton, Beaune, Gevrey-Chambertin, Nuits-St-Georges, Pommard, and Romanée-Conti. It also plays a major part in the wines of Champagne, but that's another story.

Notoriously, Burgundy is one of the most difficult wine regions of all to fathom, with wines of the same name being made by vast numbers of different growers, producers, and *négoçiants*. One thing, however, should make Burgundy the simplest of all regions to understand, and that is the fact that all its red wines (barring the very lowliest, such as Bourgogne Passe-Tout-Grains) are made from one grape and one grape only—Pinot Noir. And while it would be true to say that the gap between top-quality and low-quality burgundy is startlingly large, nowhere else in the world is the grape so successful. It may dampen your enthusiasm that old Pinot Noirs from Burgundy are often characterized by a notable smell of barnyards, but don't let it, because they taste sublime and are highly prized.

Red burgundy goes well with Coq au Vin and Beef Bourguignon; Alsace Pinot Noir with quiche and onion tart; California or Oregon Pinot Noir with broiled salmon and tuna.

Pinot Noir does well in the Loire where it produces the charming red and rosé Sancerres, and in Alsace—a region better known for its aromatic white wines—where the locals lap it up, so much so that it is rarely exported.

Being a famously bad traveler, the grape has been less triumphant outside France than other classic grape varieties, though some exciting wines are now being made in the New World. Unlike Cabernet Sauvignon, which always tastes just about the same wherever it is grown, Pinot Noir can taste very different in its various habitats. The cool climate in regions such as Oregon and Western Australia lends itself to producing vigorous wines with buckets of raspberry fruit, while New Zealand produces wines packed with cherrylike flavors.

Syrah's wines are instantly identifiable by oodles of pepper and spice on the nose, combined with plenty of blackberries and plums. Its wines are packed with tannin and so have the ability to age for decades.

s y r a h

Syrah dominates the northern Rhône in the same way that Grenache dominates the southern Rhône, and is responsible for producing such famous wines as the full-bodied Cornas, Côte Rôtie, and Hermitage, and the lighter Crozes-Hermitage and Saint Joseph.

The grape almost certainly originated in the Middle East and was brought by the Romans to the Rhône Valley, where it continues to produce wines of stunning concentration and full-bodied intensity. Syrah is an easy grape to grow. It produces a reliable crop, is resistant to most pests and diseases, and does especially well in poor soils and warm climates, so it is able to flourish on the precipitous granite slopes dangling above the Rhône River. Not only does Syrah rule the roost in the northern Rhône, it also plays a small but important part in Grenache territory in the southern Rhône, by adding flavor, weight, and body to the wines of Châteauneuf-du-Pape.

The variety's other great stronghold is Australia, where it first arrived in the 1830s. Since then, it has become the country's most widely planted grape and is known as Shiraz. It is either made into lip-smacking blends alongside Cabernet Sauvignon or into long-lived single varietals, the most celebrated example of which is Penfolds Grange—a powerfully intense wine to rival the finest in the world.

Although it has yet to match its success in France and Australia, Syrah is now being planted with more regularity in California—either for Rhône-style blends or single varietals. The grape is also beginning to shine brightly in both South America and South Africa.

Syrah in all its forms goes well with cassoulet and barbecued food, casseroles or roasts. Its spiciness also complements strongly flavored dishes such as pepperoni pizza.

Cabernet Franc should not be confused with Cabernet Sauvignon, compared to which it is less tannic, less acidic, less full-bodied, but more aromatic—its wines often smelling of black currant leaves. It is a small but significant component in many Bordeaux blends, while also being the predominant ingredient in one of the great wines of the world—Château Cheval Blanc.

cabernet franc

In the Médoc in Bordeaux, Cabernet Franc is very much the understudy to Cabernet Sauvignon's star performer. It is grown not only to boost the flavor of its near namesake in the blends, but also, because it ripens earlier, as its substitute in the event that the lead performer is indisposed by the weather. Cabernet Franc takes a far more prominent role in nearby St. Émilion, where most wines are blended from Cabernet Franc and Merlot.

Its performance is also
taken more seriously in the
Loire, where it enjoys the cool
conditions, making early maturing
light red wines such as Bourgeuil, Chinon,
Saumur-Champigny, and the delightful rosé
Cabernet d'Anjou.

Even though Cabernet Sauvignon is firmly established in
California, where the benign climate means that it rarely fails, the
earlier ripening Cabernet Franc continues to be grown there in small
amounts as a flavor-boosting backup. It is also used in the region's Bordeaux-
style Meritage wines, and there is a scattering of producers who make single
varietals from it, as there are in Australia.

Cabernet Franc can also be found in modest amounts in Argentina, New York
State, Washington State, New Zealand, and in Friuli, in northeastern Italy,
where, misleadingly, it is sometimes labeled simply as Cabernet.

barbera

Barbera thrives in warm to hot climates, producing wines high in fruit and acidity, and low in tannin. One of the most productive varieties in Italy, it is eclipsed in terms of quality if not ubiquity by the grandees Nebbiolo and Sangiovese.

Rather than making great wines, it makes solid, everyday drinking wines that are purple-colored with good acidity and plenty of chewy, raisiny fruit. Barbera's wines need little time to mature, and their low tannin levels mean that they are invariably softly quaffable, and always a pleasure to drink, without ever reaching the heights enjoyed by its two big rivals.

Barbera's main homes are Piedmont, Lombardy, and Emilia-Romagna in northern Italy; its best-known wines are Barbera d'Alba, Barbera d'Asti—both robust and full-bodied—and in combination with other varieties—Barbera del Monferrato.

Barbera is also extremely versatile, and is capable of making rosés and sparkling wines, some of which can be sweet. But despite its undoubted qualities, its popularity appears to be on the wane in Italy—in several areas it is giving way to other varieties.

Farther afield, in hotter regions, Barbera's high alcohol and good acidity levels make it an ideal variety for blending, and it appears in Argentina, California (where it is increasingly being planted in the San Joaquin Valley), former Yugoslavia, South America, and Australia.

Barbera's high natural acidity means that its wines go especially well with rich food, such as dishes with creamy sauces, as well as pasta, cold cuts, or roasted vegetables.

Carignan is still, just, France's most widely grown red grape, making dark, hefty wines that are high in both alcohol and tannin. It never makes great wine, but never makes bad wine either: at its best it is fruity and spicy, at its worst, inoffensive and dull.

carignan

Carignan originated in the Cariñena area of Aragón in northern Spain, where it continues to make fairly dreary full-bodied table wine. Although it is an integral part of the wines of Rioja, adding color to that region's wines, its main home in Spain is Catalonia, where it is also chiefly used for blending.

Being a late-ripener, Carignan does well in hot climates, and it has long dominated Languedoc-Roussillon, especially in Aude, Hérault, Gard, and Pyrénées-Orientales. These days, however, it is no longer in fashion, and many of its vines are being uprooted and replanted with more popular varieties.

Although most of its wines end up as simple *vin de table*, Carignan does play an important part in the blends that make up such well-regarded French country wines as Corbières, Fitou, Minervois, and the Provençal rosés. Its regular blending partners are Cinsault in the western Midi and Grenache in the eastern Midi.

Carignan is extremely well-traveled and continues to be grown in such diverse countries as Algeria, Argentina, Chile, Italy, Israel, Mexico, and Uruguay. It probably produces more red wine than any other variety, though rarely as a single varietal, which is why its name is less familiar than others.

Incredibly, Carignan was once the most widely grown variety in California, until a gum-chewing grape called Cabernet Sauvignon hit town...

All red Beaujolais, be it the grandest top cru
or the humblest Beaujolais Nouveau,
is made solely from unblended Gamay.

g a m a y

Although Beaujolais—in the south of Burgundy—is Gamay's main home, the grape is also grown with considerable success in the Loire, where it makes wines such as Anjou Rosé, Anjou Gamay, and Gamay de Touraine, which is often referred to—unfairly—as poor man's Beaujolais. Switzerland, too, grows a considerable amount of Gamay, most frequently blending it with Pinot Noir. In the Mâconnais and the Côte Chalonnaise in Burgundy, Pinot Noir is also used as its blending partner in the easy-drinking Bourgogne Passe-Tout-Grains, adding body and depth.

Gamay makes light, fresh, and fruity red wines packed with the juicy flavors of peaches, cherries, and berries. Typically, its wines are high in acid, low in tannin, and sometimes lacking in depth, but they are invariably eminently quaffable and are one of the few red wines that benefit from being lightly chilled, perfect for summer drinking.

Gamay is at its best when drunk young, and only the highest quality Beaujolais from fine years should be left to mature. Posters declaring *Le Beaujolais Nouveau est arrivé* is a familiar sight

every November, when, on the third Thursday of the month, that year's vintage of Beaujolais is released for immediate consumption. In good vintages this is a charming frivolity to be enjoyed uncritically with friends: in bad vintages it is an acidic public-relations stunt best avoided.

The light red wines from Beaujolais and the Loire are the ideal reds to take on a picnic: they need no particular care and attention, such as decanting, and their soft fruitiness makes them an undemanding pleasure to drink.

Gamay goes well with salads and cold cuts,

and is just right with roasted duck, veal, or chicken.

Perhaps surprisingly, it is also perfect with grilled tuna.

g r e n a c h e

The world's second most-planted red variety, Grenache is the primary grape of the southern Rhône's Châteauneuf-du-Pape and is one of the ingredients of Spain's finest wine, Vega Sicilia.

Grenache produces pale wines that are high in alcohol with pleasant hints of sweetness, and which are ideal for blending with other varieties such as Cinsault, Carignan, Mourvèdre, and Syrah. It is especially successful in producing rosés, because of its low tannin and fruity flavor.

In France, Grenache is grown mainly in Languedoc-Roussillon and the southern Rhône, where it provides up to 80 percent of the Châteauneuf-du-Pape blend, as well as being the dominant variety in the wines of Gigondas and the region's sought-after rosés such as Tavel, Lirac, Côtes du Rhône, and Côtes du Ventoux.

In Roussillon it helps make some of the great sweet wines—known as *Vins Doux Naturels*—such as Banyuls and Rivesaltes.

A top-quality Châteauneuf-du-Pape should be drunk with hefty meat dishes or strong cheese.

Grenache is Spain's most widespread red grape. Known there as Garnacha, it is an important part of the Rioja blend, where it softens Tempranillo's rougher edges. Unlike France, there are producers in Navarra who like to use Grenache by itself, to make soft, drinkable wines notably high in alcohol.

Plenty of Grenache is grown in Australia, especially in the Barossa Valley, where much of it goes into jug wines, and it is becoming increasingly popular in California where it is used in Rhône-style blends.

malbec

Malbec ripens early and produces soft wines low in tannin and acidity that are marked by spicy blackberry flavors. It was once an integral part of Bordeaux's blended red wines, but has fallen out of favor recently, often being regarded as no better than a poor man's Merlot.

Although Malbec blends perfectly with Cabernet Sauvignon, nowadays in Bordeaux—where it is known as Cot or Pressac—it is seen as having had its day. In fact, the region's only areas that still regard it with any kind of respect are Bourg and Blaye—where the vineyards are more or less divided equally between Malbec, Cabernet Sauvignon, and Merlot—and St Émilion.

Elsewhere in France, Malbec manages to cling on in the Loire, where wine makers blend it with other varieties, such as Gamay and Cabernet Franc.

The variety is popular in the Americas. Producers in California continue to use Malbec in the old Bordeaux manner, blending it with the traditional varieties of Cabernet Sauvignon, Merlot, and Petit Verdot in their Meritage wines. It is grown with some success in Chile, while the wine makers of Argentina—where it is the third most-planted variety—are more adventurous, making highly successful single varietal wines from the grape, probably the only region in the world to do so.

The grape is still favored in Cahors in southwestern France, where—known as Auxerrois—it is part of the region's celebrated "black wine," comprising up to 70 percent of the blend, which also includes Merlot and Tannat.

mourvèdre

Originally from Catalonia in Spain—where it is called Monastrell, Mourvèdre is now most associated with the south of France, where it plays its part in making the solid, fruity, everyday drinking wines of the region that are, as yet, rarely exported.

In the southern Rhône it is one of thirteen permitted varieties used in the Grenache-based blend that makes Châteauneuf-du-Pape, adding color, spice, and structure to the wine.

Of the many southern French wines to which Mourvèdre adds its fresh fruit flavors, the best known are Bandol (which must comprise at least 50 percent), Cassis, Corbières, Côtes du Roussillon, Côte du Rhône-Villages, and Palette. In most of these wines, Mourvèdre is blended with Cinsault, Syrah, Carignan, or Grenache, and it must be admitted that it struggles to escape the shadows of such varieties.

Mourvèdre's wines have a blackberry scent and are peppery and spicy on the palate, but their chewiness and high tannin content mean that they are best when blended with other varieties, and it battles to find an identity of its own.

As Monastrell, it is Spain's second most important black grape after Garnacha (Grenache), being well-suited to the warm climate and making the big, heavy reds and rosés of Valencia and Alicante.

Also known as Mataro, Mourvèdre can be found in both California, where some interesting single varietal wines are being made, and in Australia. It is also used to make rough local wine in Algeria.

nebbiolo

Italy's answer to Syrah, Nebbiolo makes the big, dark, tannic wines of Barolo and Barbaresco in the northwestern region of Piedmont, its name deriving from the *nebbia*, the fog that creeps over the Piedmontese hills.

Usually regarded as Italy's finest wines, Barolo and Barbaresco both spend regulated periods in oak barrels before being released for sale. Barolo is seen as the more robust and long-lived of these two massive wines, while Barbaresco is considered more elegant and refined: neither of them are cheap.

In addition to Barolo and Barbaresco, other wines made from the variety include Gattinara, Ghemme, and Spanna, the latter usually a blend of other varieties, too, thus making them gentler and more approachable than the big two.

The grape's wines are rich, full-bodied, chewy, and tannic. Deep in color, the wines are intense and complex, and often identifiable by their aromas of violets, raspberries, prunes, and chocolate. They usually require plenty of aging, although some producers are experimenting with modern-style wines that are softer and more approachable, and which require less aging.

Nebbiolo's wines are invariably high in alcohol, usually 13 percent or over: and are certainly neither for the faint-hearted nor the aperitif wine drinker.

Although it can produce wines of striking intensity and is recognized as one of the world's finest varieties, Nebbiolo is scarcely grown anywhere other than northwestern Italy, although some enterprising wine makers are trying it in California.

Barolo and Barbaresco go especially well with game like venison and hare, and are hard to beat as accompaniments to a winter's Sunday roast.

Although the nuances and subtleties of the wonderful liquid
that is red wine are endless, the essential truth is
that it is no more than the fermented juice of the humble grape,
gathered from fruit farms known as vineyards.

tempranillo

Tempranillo is to Spain what Cabernet Sauvignon is to France; it puts the grit into the country's most highly regarded red wines, most famously as the major component of Rioja.

Tempranillo has good color and fine aging potential. With few aromas of its own, it usually smells more of the oak it is aged in, although it can give off the odd whiff of strawberries, leather, tobacco, toffee, and spice.

Tempranillo is found throughout Spain, and although it is sometimes made into single varietal wines, it is usually blended with other varieties. In its strongholds of Rioja Alta and Rioja Alavesa, for example, it is blended with Garnacha, Mazuelo, Graciano, and Viura. In Ribera del Duero, combined with the varieties that produce claret in Bordeaux, it makes Spain's finest wine—Vega Sicilia. The major red variety in Valdepeñas and La Mancha (where it is known as Cencibel), it is also grown in Costers del Segre, Utiel-Requena, Navarra, Somontano, and Penedès.

Tempranillo in the form of Rioja goes especially well with rich meat dishes such as casseroles, roasted duck, goose, and lamb, as well as with simpler fare, such as spaghetti bolognese and lasagne.

Tempranillo is most closely associated with Spain, but it can also be found in the Midi in France, in Portugal—where, known as Roriz, it is one of the many varieties used in the production of port—and in South America, especially in the Mendoza region of Argentina.

Sangiovese is the major grape behind such celebrated Italian wines as Chianti, Brunello di Montalcino, and Vino Nobile di Montepulciano.

sangiovese

Along with Nebbiolo, Sangiovese is regarded as one of the two top red grapes in Italy, and is the most widely planted red grape in the country. Sangiovese's stronghold is in the central and southern regions of Italy, but despite the grape's high reputation, it must be said that the quality of its wines can vary dramatically, largely because so many different clones of the variety exist.

However, whatever its perceived shortcomings elsewhere might be, Sangiovese does, unquestionably, make the finest red wines of Tuscany. It is here that Chianti is made, with Sangiovese providing up to 90 percent of the blend. Chianti Classico is the highest quality Chianti, and at its best should taste of fresh herbs and cherries.

Chianti is a good partner for most simple chicken dishes and, inevitably, goes perfectly with pastas and pizzas.

Sangiovese also provides up to 80 percent of the Vino Nobile di Montepulciano blend, while under its pseudonym, Brunello, it is left unblended, making what is in effect a single varietal wine—Brunello di Montalcino, a big, dark wine with plenty of tannin.

In addition to its role in such traditional Tuscan wines, Sangiovese is also an important component (along with Cabernet Sauvignon and Merlot) in making the more modern wines known as the "Super Tuscans." Owing to the fact that non-indigenous grapes are used, such wines remained unclassified for many years, until the authorities could ignore them no longer. They now enjoy their own classification with prices to match.

Sangiovese doesn't stray much outside Italy, although there are some plantings of the variety in the Mendoza province of Argentina and in California.

cinsault

The fourth most planted variety in France, Cinsault is grown mainly in Languedoc-Roussillon where it is highly productive, making wines that are high in acidity and low in tannin.

Cinsault is used chiefly in blends, providing smoothness, spice, perfume, and fruit, although some single varietal rosés are made, too. In Languedoc-Roussillon (notably in Aude, Hérault, and Gard), it is usually blended with Carignan or Grenache, and in the southern Rhône—where it produces deeper-colored, more concentrated wines—it is frequently blended with Mourvèdre, Grenache, or Syrah. One of the thirteen approved grape varieties used in making Châteauneuf-du-Pape, Cinsault is also an obligatory ingredient in the basic Côtes du Rhône-Villages.

Its high productivity led Cinsault to be widely planted in South Africa, where, for some reason, it is sometimes known as Hermitage. South Africa's own variety, called Pinotage, is a cross between Cinsault and Pinot Noir.

The grape blends especially well with Cabernet Sauvignon and Syrah, a combination that has proved particularly successful in southern France, Australia, and Lebanon where, most famously, it is used at Château Musar.

petit verdot

Petit Verdot makes full-bodied wines, noted for their depth of color and spicy, peppery characteristics.

Petit Verdot is a high-quality grape that is not dissimilar to Syrah in its deep color and peppery spiciness. It is little seen, though, outside Bordeaux, where it has long been used as a sort of vinous monosodium glutamate, adding a bit of zip to the quartet of Cabernet Sauvignon, Merlot, Malbec, and Cabernet Franc by enhancing the blend's color, flavor, and tannin.

When used in such fashion, it usually comprises as little as 2–3 percent of the blend and certainly never more than 10 percent. It is used chiefly in the southern Médoc, where the soil produces light wines that are more in need of an extra dash of flavor than are the wines of the northern Médoc.

The grape is used in a similar manner in places such as California and Chile, adding oomph to blended wines.

p i n o t a g e

Pinotage is regarded as South Africa's own grape variety, having been developed there in 1925 as a cross between Pinot Noir and Cinsault. Even the name Pinotage is a hybrid, being a cross between Pinot Noir and Hermitage, the South African name for Cinsault.

South Africa remains its main home, although there are also plantings in California and scatterings elsewhere.

Pinotage wines are invariably deep purple in color and are often characterized on the nose by remarkably unenticing whiffs of burned rubber.

When it is on form, Pinotage can make wines of freshness and fruit, marked by raspberrylike flavors, but all too frequently it is one-dimensional and flat. Often tannic and chewy, Pinotage is sometimes compared to Syrah, although it lacks much of that grape's style and panache. Styles vary between fruity wines designed to be drunk young and full-bodied wines that need aging; in either event, despite its qualities and its individuality, Pinotage remains an acquired taste.

Drink Pinotage with casseroles and roast meats, and richly sauced dishes.

zinfandel

Zinfandel is known as California's own grape, being the region's only indigenous variety and its most widely planted. It is believed to be related to the little-known Primitivo grape found in Italy.

California remains Zinfandel's favored home, but it is being grown with increasing success in Australia, South America, and South Africa. Zinfandel produces wines similar to those of Cabernet Sauvignon, albeit with higher levels of alcohol and softer tannins, which may be drunk young, or allowed to develop with age.

The range of wines produced by Zinfandel is bewildering: as well as top-quality, full-bodied red wine, it makes semi-sweet white wine, "blush" wine, jug wine, sparkling wine, and even fortified wine.

Most commercially successful are the so-called "white Zinfandels" (which are usually pink), blended wines that may include other grapes, too, such as the white variety Muscat. The resulting semisweet wines are the closest anyone has come to creating alcoholic cotton candy in liquid form, and are best avoided.

Drink the big red Zinfandels with barbecued food, chili con carne, or roasted lamb.

f o r t i f i e d
w i n e s

Port is made by adding brandy to partially fermented red wine, thus stopping its fermentation and leaving the wine sweet, rich, and high in alcohol.

Vintage port is made only in exceptional years, spending two years in wood before being bottled, after which it can take up to 20 years to mature, remaining at its peak for a further 20 years before spending the next 20 years in a gentle decline. By the time it is ready to drink, it will have a sediment and will thus need decanting.

Tawny ports are blended wines that spend anything from 10-40 years maturing in cask before bottling, by which stage they are ready for consumption. The sediment is left in the barrel, so no decanting is required. They make excellent companions to fruitcake and cookies, and are the new fashionable accompaniment, chilled, with chocolate desserts. There are other hybrid forms of port such as Vintage Character, Crusted, and Late Bottled Vintage.

The recent fine port vintages are 1903, 1966, 1970, 1975, 1977, 1983, 1985, 1994, and 1997. In some years a vintage might not be considered as important and will be declared by only a few port houses.

The fortified wine madeira comes from the Portuguese island of Madeira located 400 miles off the coast of Morocco. During the eighteenth century, the indifferent wine produced here was often used as ballast on long sea voyages, during which it was found that the double crossing of the equator greatly reduced the wine's period of maturation. Nowadays the fermented wine is effectively "cooked" to replicate the heat of the sea voyages before it is fortified.

There are four types of madeira wine, ranging from the very dry to the very sweet: Sercial, Verdelho, Bual, and Malmsey. The driest of the madeiras goes well with soup, the slightly sweeter ones with cookies, while the richest of all go excellently with old-fashioned, very sweet desserts such as pecan pie.

Port and madeira may seem old-fashioned, but they are making a comeback and are highly enjoyable.

vintages

Differences between each wine are caused by the soil, the grapes, the way in which it was made, and above all by the weather. In New World wine regions such as California or Australia, blessed with constant temperatures and clement weather, variations between different years are less pronounced than they are in Europe. There, although poor vintages are becoming rarer owing to improved wine technology, a late frost, hailstorms, or lack of sunshine can mean the difference between success and failure for a vintage.

If a blend of two or more vintages is used, the wine will be known as non-vintage or NV, and will show no date on the label, as is often the case with inexpensive wines.

The listing of a vintage date on a label must not be taken as a guarantee of the quality of that wine—except with fine wines—but rather as simply a matter of record and a note of the wine's age.

Top red wines can take from 5–25 years to mature, although nowadays there is a trend among wine makers to produce wine for relatively early drinking.

Recent fine vintages for red Bordeaux include 1982, 1983, 1985, 1986, 1988, 1989, 1990, 1995, 1996, and 1998.

Recent fine vintages for red burgundy include 1985, 1988, 1989, 1990, 1993, 1995, 1996, 1997, and 1999.

aging

Most top-quality red wines are aged in oak
barrels prior to bottling, allowing them to mature
and to reach their full potential. They become
less tannic, smoother, and more complex,
characteristics that are further enhanced by
subsequent aging in bottles.

No wood is as good for aging wine as oak, with
great differences being achieved by the size of
the barrel, the type of oak used (usually *limousin*
or *tronçin*), and by whether it is old oak or new
oak, or a combination of the two. New oak
contains vanillin, which gives wines that have
been in barrel for any length of time a noticeable
aroma of vanilla.

Some producers prefer not to use oak, because
they feel that it imparts too much flavor to their
wines, so they use stainless steel instead. Other
producers feel that oak is essential, while some
even use oak chips as a quicker, but less
satisfactory, method of imparting the unique
flavor associated with oak.

Laying down is the practice of storing mid- to top-quality red wines and ports from the time of their purchase when young until their maturity, after which time they might be consumed or sold.

Quality, rarity, and aging potential are the main factors that influence a wine's lasting value, all of which should be considered when starting to invest in wine.

The best way to buy fine wines is when they are offered *en primeur*, where each spring following the vintage, producers reveal the opening price for their new wines. Customers pay in advance for these wines, and take delivery of them, after bottling, some 18 months later.

Port tends to hold its value well, largely because vintages are not declared every year.

Some smart investors buy two cases of each wine, one to drink and one to sell. In this way, after the initial investment, your cellar can become self-financing.

Most less expensive wines are not meant to be laid down and will do nothing except lose their fruit and vivacity if they are kept too long.

A good restaurant should pride itself on having carefully chosen good-quality wines, and you should feel confident about ordering them.

When the bottle is brought to you, check that it is exactly what you ordered (vintage, château, etc.), and make sure it is opened at the table.

Check that the wine's temperature is satisfactory. If the red is too cool, ask for it to be put near a source of heat for 15 minutes or so.

Don't be hurried into tasting the red wine: wait until you have a clear palate; just "nose" the glass or ask the wine waiter to come back.

Remember that some restaurants declare in their lists that, if a certain vintage is unavailable, they will substitute it with the subsequent one. This is acceptable for a simple Bulgarian Cabernet Sauvignon, say, but not for finer wines; for example, you would not want a fine 1983 Bordeaux replaced by one from the less successful 1984 vintage.

When in doubt about the choices facing you, ask the wine waiter for his or her advice: after all, that is what they are there for.

wine in
restaurants

food and wine

There is only one rule to bear in mind when matching wine with food, and that is don't be afraid to experiment. Trial and error is the only way to find that perfect pairing where wine and food combine in harmony, each enhancing the other. Generally speaking, the lighter the dish, the lighter the wine should be, and the heavier the dish, the heavier the wine. But everyone's taste differs, and while you should always bear in mind the experience of those who have trodden this path before you, the only way to find out what you like is to try it for yourself. The pairings listed below should be considered as no more than suggestions and ideas to set you on your way; wine was created to accompany food, and you will be surprised at some of the unlikely combinations that succeed. Be brave and enjoy!

Aperitifs If you're bored with white wine, try a well-chilled Beaujolais or red Sancerre.

Beef

BEEF STEW A robust red such as a Côte Rôtie or Hermitage from the Rhône, an Australian Shiraz or a top-quality Rioja.
BEEF STROGANOFF Any red of character, such as Barolo, Barbaresco or a robust southern French.

HAMBURGERS A young, fruity Chianti or Beaujolais would work well, as would a Chilean Merlot or Cabernet Sauvignon.

ROASTED BEEF Any good red wine.

STEAK A New World Cabernet Sauvignon is hard to beat.

Casseroles

CASSOULET This wonderful bean-and-sausage casserole is best accompanied by a sturdy French country wine such as Cahors, Madiran, or Corbières.

CHOUCROUTE GARNI A lightish Pinot Noir or a fruity Beaujolais.

LAMB CASSEROLE You don't need anything amazing—a mid range New World Cabernet or Merlot won't let you down.

Charcuterie

HAM AND PROSCIUTTO Classy Italian reds or Riojas would fit the bill.

PÂTÉS AND TERRINES It depends on what they are made from, but any smooth, soft red should do.

SALAMI Something spicy.

SAUSAGES Any medium- to full-bodied red wine will do.

Cheese

BLUE CHEESE (such as Gorgonzola or Roquefort) Vintage port is traditional, but why not try an Italian Barbera or Chilean Cabernet Sauvignon instead?

GOAT CHEESE White wine is best, but Beaujolais will also make an acceptable partner.

HARD CHEESE (such as Cheddar or Parmesan) A medium-quality red Bordeaux or tawny port.

SOFT CHEESE (such as Brie) Almost any red wine will do, but nothing fancy.

Chicken

CHICKEN POT PIE Try a Chilean Cabernet Sauvignon or Merlot.

COQ AU VIN Red burgundy is the obvious (and most authentic) choice for this classic chicken dish.

FRIED CHICKEN a good quality Côtes du Rhône would go well, as would a mellow Merlot.

ROASTED CHICKEN Almost any red wine. (To save time and effort—add a large glass of red wine and one of broth poured around the bird in the roasting pan—it will keep the flesh deliciously moist, and provide a tasty gravy.)

Chili con carne Nothing fancy; a simple Chianti or Valpolicella is best.

Chinese food White wine for preference, but you could do worse than a Zinfandel or Beaujolais.

Cookies Médium-dry madeira such as Bual or Rainwater or a perhaps a tawny port would work well.

Duck

GRILLED DUCK BREASTS Zinfandel or an oaky Rioja.

ROASTED DUCK A full-bodied red such as Barolo, Hermitage, Châteauneuf-du-Pape, or Australian Shiraz.

Egg dishes

OMELETS Eggs are notoriously difficult with wine, but a ham or cheese omelet wouldn't object to being washed down by a fruity Beaujolais.

QUICHE AND ONION TART Something light and simple, an Alsace Pinot Noir perhaps.

Fish

GRILLED SALMON It may surprise you, but some fish dishes do go well with red wine, and an Oregon Pinot Noir would be perfect here.

TUNA STEAK A top-class Beaujolais or an Oregon Pinot Noir would be great.

Game
Meat such as quail, pheasant, wild duck, venison, or boar, whether roasted or casseroled, need hefty wines such as Californian Cabernet Sauvignon, Barolo, a fine Rhône, or Rioja.

Goose This deserves a good claret or a red burgundy.

Goulash A full-bodied red from Hungary would be most appropriate, or failing that, a decent Cabernet or Merlot from Bulgaria.

Greek food Greek wine obviously, but stick to white for the first courses. Or you could have Bulgarian Cabernet Sauvignon or Lebanese Château Musar for moussaka and lamb kabobs.

Ham (*See* Chacuterie)

Hamburgers (*See* Beef)

Indian food Beer is the usual choice, but failing that, try a well-chilled light red from the Loire.

Lamb
LAMB CHOPS Any soft, mellow red, like an Australian Cabernet/Shiraz perhaps, an Alsace Pinot Noir, or a Rioja.
ROASTED LAMB This classic dish deserves a fine red Bordeaux or New World Cabernet Sauvignon.

Meatballs A red with a bit of edge such as Crozes-Hermitage or Australian Shiraz.

Mexican food A spicy Zinfandel is needed here, or a peppery Rhône such as St Joseph or Cornas.

Nuts Madeira or tawny port.

Organ Meats
CALF LIVER Something soft like a mature Beaujolais or oaky Rioja are the best accompaniments.
KIDNEY Any red with flavor and structure like a red Bordeaux, Rhône, or Rioja.
OXTAIL You will need a wine with bags of flavor like a Californian or Australian Cabernet, a South African Pinotage, or a Châteauneuf-du-Pape.

Onion tart (*See* Egg dishes)

Pasta
PESTO Any soft red, with Chianti or Zinfandel working especially well.
RED SAUCES Any Italian red, but ideally a Chianti.
WHITE SAUCES Ditto.

Picnics If you take red wine on a picnic, open it beforehand and recork it—even decant it and rebottle it. (This means that you can taste it beforehand to check that it is okay and clear of sediment, and that you don't have to worry about forgetting the corkscrew. It also allows instant access to alcohol, so that that special moment is not lost)

Pizza A Chianti or any other Italian red wine will do.

Pork
ROASTED PORK Any good red wine goes well with pork, but, just for the fun of it, why not try one from Portugal or New Zealand?

CHOPS Almost any red—try and Old World or a New World Pinot Noir.

Quiche (*See* Egg dishes)

Risotto Any red from Italy or the Loire.

Roasted or stuffed peppers These need something Mediterranean like an Italian red, southern French, or even Lebanese.

Salad It depends on the dressing and on what is in it, but a light red should certainly do the trick.

Sausages (*See* Chacuterie)

Soup A Sercial Madeira makes a change from the traditional dry sherry.

Steak (*See* Beef)

Tapas It should be sherry, but any Spanish red is just as authentic.

Thai Beaujolais or red Loire.

Turkey
ROASTED TURKEY This most boring of dishes needs a good quality red to take your mind off it.
COLD TURKEY So does this.

Veal
ALLA PARMIGIANA Any good red burgundy or decent Italian.
ROASTED VEAL Something soft and mature is best, like an old claret, red burgundy, or Rioja.
MILANESE Something Italian.
OSSO BUCO A soft, silky Californian Pinot Noir, or juicy Chilean Cabernet is best.

Vegetable kabobs Good-quality Beaujolais or southern French.

quality classifications

Wine laws are strict, and their purpose is twofold: to protect the producer, by making sure his region's reputation isn't undermined by the unscrupulous practices of some rogue, and to protect the consumer by guaranteeing the basic quality and character of the wine.

In general, France's stringent *Appellation d'Origine Contrôlée* (AOC) laws give a guarantee to a wine's origins and authenticity as to grape variety, but without guaranteeing quality. The categories below AOC are *Vin Délimité de Qualité Supérieure* (VDQS), *Vin de Pays*, and *Vin de Table*: these are for lower-quality wines and have less rigid restrictions as to their production.

Italy has a similar system, the *Denominazione di Origine Controllata* (DOC), although many top producers consider it too restrictive and make great wines that are obliged to be classified as *Vino da Tavola*. A new classification, *Indicazione Geografica Tipica* (IGT), has been introduced to alleviate some of the confusion.

In Bordeaux the top 60 wines in the Médoc are classified as *Grands Crus Classé* or Classified Growths, and represent the aristocracy of the thousands of Bordeaux châteaux in five divisions. One step lower come the *Crus Bourgeois* or Bourgeois Growths, still excellent wines and usually good value. In Burgundy, a classification of *Premiers Crus* and *Grands Crus* identify the best vineyards, again based on location.

Spain and Italy designate their wines *Reserva* or *Riserva* to indicate a certain period in oak, a treatment usually confined to only the best wines, unlike the French whose categories relate to location.

In 1983 the United States set up the American Viticultural Area (AVA) system, in an attempt to emulate France's AOC laws, but like the rest of the New World, American wines remain free from the rigid restrictions that govern European wines, something which is often more than made up for by producers giving extraordinarily detailed information on back labels.

Virtually every European wine-growing region
has its own rules as to which grapes may be used, and
where and by what method they might be grown and vinified:
where such regulations do not exist, individual producers
often create a structure of their own.

storing

It pays to look after your wine properly, be it half a dozen bottles of inexpensive wine from the supermarket or a case of red Bordeaux that needs time to mature. Don't panic if you haven't got a cellar: a bottle of wine is like a baby, far sturdier than you might imagine. So long as you store the bottles on their sides (to make sure the corks don't dry out), and avoid exposing them to long periods of fluctuating temperatures, damp, strong aromas, bright lights, and vibrations, you can be certain that the wine will remain in good shape.

serving and decanting

Remove the capsule from the top of the bottle with a foil-cutter, or a strong thumbnail. Use a decent corkscrew to remove the cork—I favor the Screwpull.

Mature red wines and vintage ports are liable to leave a sediment and should be decanted (a plastic funnel, coffee filter, and a clean empty bottle are just as effective as anything grander), a process that also helps the wines to "breathe" and release their flavors.

Red wines are best served at room temperature, although lighter ones such as those from Beaujolais and the Loire can be delicious chilled. In company, taste the wine first to check that it is okay before filling your guests' glasses.

Fill no more than a quarter of your glass and look at the wine. It should be clear and bright without any cloudiness or haziness. Holding the stem, swirl the glass around to release the bouquet. Put your nose to the glass and inhale deeply; the wine should smell clean and fresh. Almost anything that might be wrong with a wine can be detected on the nose, by odors of mustiness perhaps, or dampness. Take a mouthful of the wine, drawing air into the mouth as you do so. Roll the liquid around your tongue and then spit or swallow. What is it like? Is it sweet or dry, light or full-bodied? Does it remind you of anything? The taste of a fine wine remains in the mouth, and its many components—its acidity, alcohol, fruit, and tannin—should have combined so pleasantly that you want nothing more than to take another sip.

glossary

Acid/acidity Acids occur naturally in wine. They're crucial in giving it character and structure, and help it age.

Aroma The varietal smell of a wine.

Balance A wine's harmonious combination of acids, tannins, alcohol, fruit, and flavor.

Blind tasting A tasting of wines at which the labels and shapes of the bottles are concealed from the tasters.

Bodega (Spanish) Winery.

Body The weight and structure of a wine.

Bouquet The complex scent of a wine that develops as it matures.

Cantina (Italian) Winery or cellar.

Carafe Simple decanter without a stopper.

Cave (French) Cellar.

Cellar book A useful way of noting what wines you have bought, from where, and at what price, as well as recording when you consumed them and what they tasted like.

Cepa (Spanish) Term for vine variety.

Cépage (French) Term for vine variety.

Chai (French) Place for storing wine.

Chambrer From *chambre*, the French word for "room," the practice of allowing a wine gradually to reach room temperature before drinking.

Château (French) Term for a wine-growing property—chiefly used in Bordeaux.

Claret Term given to the red wines of Bordeaux in Europe.

Climat (French) Term for a particular vineyard—chiefly used in Burgundy.

Colheita (Portuguese) Vintage.

Clos (French) Enclosed vineyard.

Corked Condition, indicated by a musty odor, where a wine has been contaminated by a faulty cork.

Cosecha (Spanish) Vintage.

Côte (French) Hillside of vineyards.

Cradle A wicker basket in which some fancy restaurants present a bottle of undecanted red wine—usually a burgundy—to the table.

Cru (French) Growth or vineyard.

Cru Classé (French) Classed Growth, especially those 61 red wines of the Médoc (and one from the Graves) in Bordeaux that were graded into five categories determined by price (and therefore, in theory, quality) in 1855. Elsewhere in Bordeaux, similar classifications followed for the red wines of Graves in 1953 and for St. Émilion in 1954 (revised in 1969 and 1985).

Cuvée (French) Blended or specially selected wine.

Decanter Glass container with a stopper into which red wines and ports are decanted to allow them to breathe or to separate them from their sediment.

Domaine (French) Property or estate.

Fermentation Natural process whereby grape juice turns into wine.

Fortified wine A wine—such as port, sherry, madeira, or *Vin Doux Naturel*—to which alcohol has been added, either in order to stop it from fermenting before all its sugars are turned into alcohol (thus maintaining its sweetness) or simply to strengthen it.

Grand Cru (French) Term for top-quality wine, used especially in Bordeaux and Burgundy.

Horizontal tasting A tasting of several different wines from the same vintage.

Meritage Term first coined in 1988 for California wines blended from the classic red varieties of Bordeaux.

Négociant (French) Wine

merchant, shipper, or grower who buys wine or grapes in bulk from several sources before vinifying and or bottling the wine himself.

Non-vintage (NV) Term applied to any wine that is a blend of two or more different vintages—notably champagne and port.

Nose The overall sense given off by a wine on being smelled. It is not just the wine's scent; the nose also conveys information about the wine's well-being.

Oak A great deal of wine is aged in oak barrels, something which is usually typified by whiffs of vanilla or cedar.

Oxidized Term used to describe wine that has deteriorated owing to overlong exposure to air.

Phylloxera An aphidlike insect that attacks the roots of vines with disastrous results.

Punt The indentation at the bottom of a bottle, serving not only to catch any sediment but also to strengthen the bottle.

Quinta (Portuguese) Wine-growing estate.

Récolte (French) Crop or vintage.

Rosso (Italian) Red.

Rouge (French) Red.

Sediment The deposit that forms after a wine has spent a lengthy period in the bottle.

Sommelier Wine waiter.

Spittoon Receptacle into which one expectorates wine at a wine tasting.

Tannin The austere acid—and necessary preservative—found in some red wines, usually young ones, which derives from grape skins and stalks combined with the oak barrels in which the wine has been aged.

Tastevin A small silver tasting dish, most commonly used in Burgundy.

Terroir (French) Literally the word means "soil" or "earth," but it also encompasses climate, drainage, position, and anything that contributes to the mystery that makes one wine taste like this, while its immediate neighbors—grown and produced in the same way—taste like that.

Tinto (Spanish/Portuguese) Red.

Ullage The amount of air in a bottle or barrel between the top of the wine and the bottom of the cork or bung.

Varietal A wine named after the grape (or its major constituent grape) from which it is made.

Variety Term for each distinctive breed of grape.

Vendange (French) Harvest or vintage.

Vendemmia (Italian) Harvest or vintage.

Vendimia (Spanish) Harvest or vintage.

Vertical tasting A tasting of several wines from the same property that all come from different vintages.

Vigneron (French) Wine grower.

Vin de pays (French) Country wine of a level higher than table wine.

Vin de table (French) Table wine.

Vin Doux Naturel (VDN) (French) A fortified wine that has been sweetened and strengthened by the addition of alcohol, either before or after fermentation has taken place.

Vin ordinaire (French) Basic wine not subject to any regulations.

Vinification Winemaking.

Vino da tavola (Italian) Table wine.

Vino de mesa (Spanish) Table wine.

Vintage Both the year of the grape harvest itself as well as the wine made from those grapes.

Viticulture Cultivation of grapes.

Weight The body and/or strength of a wine.

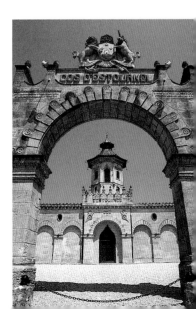

index

acknowledgements

I would like to thank Anne Ryland for coming up with the idea in the first place, and Alison Starling, Gabriella Le Grazie, Luis Peral-Aranda and Maddalena Bastianelli for making the project such an enjoyable one. I am also most grateful to Judith Murray, to David Roberts MW and to Alan Williams for his beautiful photographs, several of which were taken at the restaurant Villandry, and the wine merchant Berry Bros and Rudd Ltd, to whom also many thanks. Finally, of course, I would like to thank my wife Marina, ever patient and ever wise, and without whom...

Villandry
170 Great Portland Street
London W1N 5TB
020 7631 3131

Berry Bros & Rudd Ltd
3 St. James's Street
London SW1A 1EG
020 7390 9600

The author and publisher would also like to thank the following companies for allowing us to photograph their vineyards, wineries and cellars.

AUSTRALIA
AP Johns Cooperage, Tenuda, NSW.
d'Arenberg, McLaren Vale, South Australia
Peter Lehmann Estate, Barossa Valley, South Australia
Rockford Vineyards, Barossa Valley, South Australia

CALIFORNIA
Beringer Wine Estates, St. Helena, Napa Valley
Heitz Wine Cellars, St. Helena, Napa Valley

FRANCE
Château Belair, St. Émilion
Château Margaux, Pauillac
Maison des Vins, St. Émilion

SPAIN
Bodegas Muga, Haro
La Rioja Alta Haro